*P*asta and noodles have been enjoyed in many forms throughout Europe and Asia for centuries.

Versatile, quick and easy to prepare, they are also inexpensive. Served simply with butter and cheese or dressed with the most elaborate sauce, pasta can be right for any occasion.

The recipes included in this book mainly use dried pasta, which is both quick and convenient. For a delicious change, try substituting fresh pasta.

THE DOUGH

Pasta dough is simple to prepare. Different flavours and textures can be achieved by altering the basic ingredients just a little.

Pasta dough should have a rather dry texture and be quite firm. If the dough becomes too moist, it is difficult to work with, so knead in a little extra flour to achieve the right consistency.

Kneading is essential to make the dough elastic and easy to handle. Check after 5–10 minutes — dough is sufficiently kneaded when you make a light indentation in it with your finger and the dough springs back immediately. At this stage dough is too elastic to roll, so wrap in plastic wrap or waxed paper and leave for about 10 minutes — the dough will soften slightly and be easier to roll out.

Fresh Pasta Dough

Preparation time:
    10 minutes
Cooking time: nil
EASY

3 cups plain flour
3 eggs
1 tablespoon olive oil
3 tablespoons water

1 Sift flour into a large bowl or into a mound on a flat surface. Make a well in the centre. Whisk together eggs, oil and water.

2 Add three-quarters of the egg mixture to the flour and cut liquid through flour using two flat-bladed knives. Add remaining liquid if needed, to form a stiff dough. Knead dough for about 20 minutes until smooth and elastic. Divide dough into four pieces and use as desired.

HINT
Freeze prepared fresh pasta in freezer bags or foil for up to three months. Cook directly from the frozen state.

Making pasta

1 *Sift flour onto a flat surface. Add egg, oil and water.*

2 *Mix dough using two flat-bladed knives.*

3 *Knead dough until smooth and elastic.*

Pasta varieties, from left to right: Chickpea and Garlic, Cheese and Basil, Lemon and Pepper, Spinach, Almond, Saffron, Buckwheat, Tomato and Wholemeal Pastas

Fresh Semolina Pasta

Preparation time:
    10 minutes
Cooking time: nil
EASY

3 cups fine semolina
2 eggs
1 tablespoon olive oil
200 mL lukewarm water

1 Sift semolina into a large bowl or into a mound on a flat surface. Make a well in the centre. Whisk together eggs, oil and water.
2 Add three-quarters of the egg mixture to the semolina and cut liquid through semolina using two flat-bladed knives. Add remaining liquid if needed, to form a stiff dough. Knead dough for about 10 minutes until smooth and elastic. Divide dough into four pieces. Roll and shape as desired.

ROLLING PASTA
Pasta can be rolled by hand, which takes a little time, but for the inexperienced cook is easily managed if the pasta is rolled in small lots.

Using a pasta machine makes rolling the pasta far easier and if you have a passion for fresh pasta it is a worthwhile investment.

Rolling by Hand
Take a quarter of the dough and place it on a clean, flat, lightly floured work surface, such as a kitchen bench or table. Flatten the dough lightly with the palm of your hand.

Use a large rolling pin and roll pasta out thinly, rolling from the centre to the edge. Avoid rolling over the edge since this makes the edges paper

Perfect

PASTA

Easy-to-prepare inexpensive meals of home-
made or prepared pasta with a host of
delicious sauces.

MURDOCH BOOKS
Sydney • London • Vancouver

—MAKING PASTA—

Pasta comes in a great variety of shapes and sizes

thin and harder to handle. Keep moving rolled dough and dust board and rolling pin with extra flour if needed. After rolling, cut and shape as desired. If the pasta is not being cut or shaped immediately, cover with a clean dry tea-towel with a damp tea-towel on top. This prevents dough drying out and becoming brittle.

Rolling by Machine
Divide dough into four

pieces, and flatten lightly on a floured board.

Set the roller on the pasta machine to the widest setting and dust with a little flour.

Feed each portion of dough through the machine twice. Lay flat on a board and fold into three. Feed the folded pastry, unfolded edge first, through the machine. Feed the pasta through six times more, by which time it should have become smooth and silky in appearance.

If pasta is sticking, dust lightly with a little flour.

Change setting on machine to bring rollers one notch closer together. Feed pasta through once only — this will make the pasta thinner and longer. Set machine one notch closer and again feed pasta through. Repeat this process to the second thinnest setting — at this stage the pasta is the ideal thickness for most uses. If you prefer fine papery pasta, then roll pasta through the thinnest setting. Cut or shape as desired.

CUTTING PASTA
Ribbon-shaped Noodles
Roll sheets of pasta Swiss roll style to form a long cylinder shape. Slice into desired widths. Unravel and cook straight away or allow pasta to dry in a warm airy spot before storing. If pasta is a little too moist, dust it lightly

Rolling pasta by hand

1 Place dough on a lightly floured board and roll from the centre outwards.

2 Roll until thin and use as required.

Rolling pasta with a machine

1 Feed flattened dough through rollers.

2 Fold pasta into three.

3 Feed pasta again through rollers, reducing width until thin.

5

with flour before rolling. Rolled pasta can be fed through the cutters of a pasta machine to form long ribbons.

Lasagne or Cannelloni
Use a sharp, straight-edged knife or a sharp, fluted pastry wheel. Cut the lasagne to the same size as your lasagne dish or cut into sheets approximately 10 cm x 12 cm. Cut cannelloni into 10 cm x 12 cm sheets. These are then boiled and cooled before rolling around the filling.

Bows and Twists
To make bows: cut rolled pasta into 3 cm squares with a fluted cutter. Pinch two straight edges together to form bows.
To make twists: cut pasta into 5 cm x 2 cm lengths with a fluted pastry wheel. Cut a 2 cm slit down the top half of the strip. Pull bottom half up through cut to form a twist.

Filled Pasta
To make tortellini: cut pasta into 5 cm rounds. Place a little filling on one side of round, and lightly brush half the edge with water. Join the moist and dry edges and press firmly together to form a crescent shape. Curve the crescent around and join tips together, sealing with a little water.
To make ravioli: place a sheet of rolled pasta onto a flat surface. Spoon mounds of filling across the width and down the length of the pasta at 4 cm intervals. Lightly brush between mounds with a little water. Lay a second sheet of pasta on the top of the first pasta layer. Press firmly between the mounds. Cut between mounds into squares using a sharp knife or sharp fluted pastry wheel.

DRYING PASTA

Fresh pasta can be cooked as soon as it is made. However, if dried sufficiently, fresh pasta can be stored in the cupboard indefinitely, ready for use when required.

To dry pasta shapes: place on a flat tray lined with absorbent paper or on a wire rack, and put in a dry airy place. Turn regularly until crisp and thoroughly dry.

To dry ribbon-shaped noodles: either place loose nests of pasta on a wire rack and leave to dry or hang pasta over a broom handle or curtain rod suspended between two chairs, and leave to dry.

Cutting pasta

1 *Roll up pasta Swiss roll style.*

2 *Cut pasta into ribbon noodles.*

3 *Feed rolled pasta dough through cutting section of pasta machine.*

Shaping tortellini

1 *Cut rolled dough into rounds.*

2 *Spoon a little filling in centre.*

3 *Moisten half the edge and fold over to form a crescent.*

4 *Curve crescent around and join tips together. Seal with water.*

After pasta has thoroughly dried, store in an airtight container until ready to use.

Commercial dried pasta is, of course, readily available. It is worth trying a few different brands until you find the one you are happy with, since brands do vary slightly in texture and the time they take to cook.

COOKING PASTA

Pasta needs to be cooked properly before serving.

Fresh Plain Pasta

This can be fried and, for coffee treats, dusted with icing sugar. Mostly, however, pasta is boiled in a large amount of boiling water. Traditionally salt is added to the cooking water. This is really not necessary, as pasta has plenty of flavour, especially when combined with delicious sauces.

To cook pasta bring a large pan of water to a rapid boil. Add a little oil to prevent sticking. Add pasta and give it a stir to ensure no pasta has stuck to the base of the pan. Boil until pasta is *al dente* — firm yet tender. Drain through a colander or strainer and if cooking water is milky in appearance, then rinse pasta with some fresh hot or cold water (if the cooking water is clearish, this is unnecessary).

To re-heat, place pasta in a dish over a saucepan of simmering water for approximately 10 minutes or until warm.

Other Types of Pasta

Instant or pre-cooked lasagne and cannelloni shells save time as you can omit boiling the pasta before layering or filling. For best results, soak the pasta in warm water for 5–10 minutes before using.

Pastas that contain a filling such as ravioli or tortellini are best purchased fresh or frozen. Fresh ravioli and tortellini usually need to be boiled 5–7 minutes until tender. In frozen form they need about 15 minutes cooking.

FLAVOURED PASTAS

You can add interest and variety to your pasta dishes by substituting fresh flavoured pasta for the dried commercial varieties. The possibilities are endless and it is worth trying a few different combinations:

Tomato Pasta
Add 1 tablespoon tomato paste and 1 clove crushed garlic (optional) to egg mixture. This pasta is a lovely rich orange which, during cooking, lightens a little.

Cheese and Basil Pasta
Add ½ cup finely grated parmesan and 2 tablespoons finely chopped fresh basil to flour before mixing with egg. Delicious served tossed with a little butter as an accompaniment to a meal.

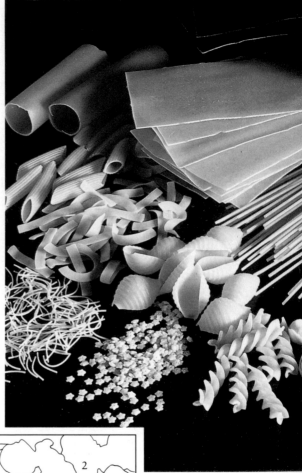

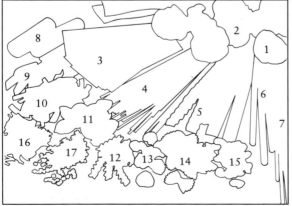

1. Fettuccine
2. Vermicelli
3. Lasagne
4. Spaghetti
5. Pappardelle
6. Rigatoni
7. Bucatini
8. Cannelloni
9. Penne
10. Tagliatelle
11. Shells
12. Fusilli

13. *Tortellini*
14. *Farfalle*
15. *Macaroni*
16. *Gramigna*
17. *Stellette*

Chickpea and Garlic Pasta
Replace 1 cup plain flour with chickpea flour, and add ½ teaspoon garlic powder to eggs. Best

served simply with a little olive oil and chopped fresh herbs or chilli.

Lemon and Pepper Pasta
Add 2 teaspoons finely grated lemon rind and 1 teaspoon coarsely ground black pepper to flour before mixing with eggs. Delicious for

seafood-filled tortellini or served with a light cream sauce.

Spinach Pasta
Cook 225 g spinach leaves until soft. Chop finely and squeeze out excess moisture to make spinach quite dry. Add to flour before adding enough egg and oil to form a dough. This beautiful green pasta is perfect for spinach lasagne or as an accompaniment to a main meal.

Wholemeal Pasta
You can use all wholemeal flour, however, the result can be a little heavy. It is often best to use half white and half wholemeal flour. The pasta may need a little extra liquid depending on the flour, in which case use chilled water. This pasta has a delicious nutty flavour and slightly heavier texture.

Buckwheat Pasta
Replace 1½ cups of the plain flour with 1½ cups of buckwheat flour.

Almond Pasta
Combine 1 cup wholemeal flour, 100 g ground almonds, 3 tablespoons icing sugar. Add 2 eggs and ¼ teaspoon almond essence and mix to form a dough.

–ESSENTIAL SAUCES–

*P*asta is generally named after the shape, not the ingredients it contains. While some shaped pastas are more suited to particular styles of dishes, you shouldn't allow this to restrict you. Try different shapes for your favourite dishes and combine with any of these delicious sauces.

Rich Meat Sauce

With a stock of this in the refrigerator or freezer, you can make up many delicious recipes.

Preparation time: 30 minutes
Cooking time: 1¾ hours
Makes 1.5 litres
EASY

4 tablespoons oil
1.5 kg minced steak
3 large onions, finely chopped
3 large green capsicums, diced
6 large cloves garlic, crushed
3 x 425 g cans whole tomatoes
3 cups tomato purée
3 x 235 g cans tomato paste
1 tablespoon dried oregano leaves
3 teaspoons dried basil leaves
½ teaspoon pepper
1½ cups red wine
4 tablespoons beef stock

1 Heat oil in a large frying pan. Add meat a little at a time and brown, stirring constantly. As each batch is cooked, remove to a bowl. Repeat with remaining meat. Add onions, capsicums and garlic to pan and slowly cook until softened.
2 Return meat to pan with remaining ingredients. Simmer, uncovered, stirring frequently for about 1½ hours, or until thickened. Serve over hot noodles or sphagetti.

Anchovy and Garlic Sauce

Preparation time: 8 minutes
Cooking time: 5 minutes
Makes 1 cup
EASY

125 g butter
4 cloves garlic, crushed
2 x 45 g cans flat anchovy fillets, undrained and coarsely chopped
2–4 tablespoons hot water
1½ cups chopped fresh parsley
pinch pepper

1 Melt butter in a small frying pan. Add garlic and cook until tender.
2 Stir in anchovies with their oil. Add water and stir to mix. Add parsley and pepper to taste.

Serve sauce tossed through hot noodles.

HINT
The salty flavour of anchovies can be mellowed by soaking them in a little milk for 30 minutes before using. Drain and use as directed in recipe.

Tuna Sauce

Preparation time: 10 minutes
Cooking time: 15 minutes
Makes 2 cups
EASY

90 g butter
1 clove garlic, crushed
250 g small mushrooms, thickly sliced
¾ cup tomato purée
1 x 185 g can tuna, drained and flaked
pinch black pepper
chopped fresh parsley to garnish

1 Heat butter in pan. Gently fry garlic for 2 minutes then remove from pan. Add mushrooms and fry, stirring gently until just softened.
2 Stir in tomato purée, tuna and pepper to taste. Cook over low heat for about 10 minutes. Serve over hot noodles garnished with parsley.

Mushroom Cream Sauce

Preparation time: 10 minutes
Cooking time: 8 minutes
Makes 2 cups
EASY

60 g butter
185 g small mushrooms, sliced
1 clove garlic, crushed
300 mL cream
1 teaspoon grated lemon rind
pinch pepper
pinch nutmeg
3 tablespoons grated parmesan cheese

1 Melt butter in a pan. Add mushrooms and gently fry for 30 seconds. Add garlic, cream, lemon rind, pepper and nutmeg to taste.
2 Stir over low heat for 1–2 minutes. Add parmesan and cook gently for 3 minutes. Serve over any shaped macaroni or ribbon noodles.
Variation: Substitute crumbled blue vein cheese for parmesan cheese.

Fresh Tomato Sauce

Preparation time: 15 minutes
Cooking time: 45 minutes
Makes 4 cups
EASY

1 tablespoon oil
2 large onions, chopped
½ cup chopped celery
2 cloves garlic, crushed
4 cups chopped peeled tomatoes
½ teaspoon dried oregano leaves or 1½ teaspoons fresh
pinch black pepper
1 teaspoon sugar
1 bay leaf

1 Heat oil in a pan. Gently fry onions and celery until onions soften. Add garlic, tomatoes, oregano, pepper to taste, sugar and bay leaf.
2 Bring to the boil, lower heat, cover and simmer for about 40 minutes. Remove bay leaf and toss sauce through hot noodles to serve.

Variation:
If you wish, add 125 g small mushrooms about 10 minutes before cooking time is finished. Mushrooms can be quartered or sliced, then gently fried in a little butter and mixed through.

Pesto

Preparation time: 10 minutes
Cooking time: nil
Makes 1½ cups
EASY

125 g parmesan, romano or pecorino cheese, cut in small cubes
2 cloves garlic
½ cup pine nuts or walnuts
1 cup tightly packed fresh basil leaves
½ cup olive oil

1 Process cheese cubes in a food processor with chopping blade until finely grated. Add garlic, nuts and basil, and process again until finely chopped.
2 With machine running, slowly pour in oil through feed tube, processing until thickened and combined. Spoon over hot cooked and drained pasta. Toss well and serve.

HINT
Pesto is best made fresh when required. As fresh basil is not available all year round, pesto can be made using flat leaf parsley, which produces a different, yet delicious sauce.

Clockwise from top left: Mushroom Cream Sauce, Fresh Tomato Sauce, and Pesto

Tagliatelle con Prosciutto

*S*ee just how versatile pasta can be — there are so many delicious ways to combine pasta with fresh meat, chicken and smallgoods from the delicatessen. *The recipes here can provide many memorable meals that will convert even the fussiest of your family to the delights of pasta.*

These dishes are examples of both European and oriental cuisine, and are for the most part quick and easy to prepare. Try one the next time you want a deliciously different meal.

Tagliatelle con Prosciutto

Preparation time: 15 minutes
Cooking time: 20 minutes
Serves 2
EASY

1 tablespoon oil
200 g tagliatelle
60 g butter
1 onion, sliced
200 g boiled ham, diced
250 g frozen peas
1 cup dry white wine
1 stock cube
1/2 cup water
2 tablespoons grated parmesan cheese

1 Bring a large pan of water and the oil to the boil. Add tagliatelle and cook for 6–8 minutes, or until firm and tender. Drain, rinse under warm water and drain again. Keep warm.
2 Heat butter in a pan. Fry onion until soft but not brown. Add ham and peas, and fry for a few minutes without browning. Pour wine over and cook until almost completely evaporated.
3 Crumble stock cube over top and add water. Bring to the boil. Add hot drained pasta. Serve topped with grated cheese.

HINT
To vary this dish, you can add 1 cup cream instead of the stock.

Spicy Tagliatelle

Preparation time: 15 minutes
Cooking time: 25 minutes
Serves 6
EASY

1 tablespoon oil
250 g each green and white tagliatelle
2 tablespoons chopped fresh parsley
4 tablespoons grated parmesan cheese

Sauce
30 g butter
1 onion, chopped
125 g peperoni or Hungarian salami, chopped
125 g button mushrooms, sliced
1/2 red capsicum, cut into thin strips
4 tablespoons dry white wine
3 tablespoons lemon juice
1 x 425 g can peeled tomatoes, chopped

1 To prepare pasta: bring a large pan of water and the oil to the boil. Add tagliatelle and cook in boiling water for 6–8 minutes, or until firm and tender. Drain, rinse under warm water and drain again. Keep warm.
2 To prepare sauce: melt butter in a frying pan. Sauté onion until soft. Add peperoni, mushrooms and capsicum. Sauté for a few minutes. Stir in wine, lemon juice and tomatoes. Bring to the boil. Reduce heat and simmer 5 minutes.
3 Return pasta to pan. Add parsley and parmesan. Toss well and serve immediately.

Oriental Beef and Noodles

Preparation time: 25 minutes
Cooking time: 30 minutes
Serves 4
EASY

1 tablespoon oil
500 g fettuccine

Sauce
4 tablespoons oil
500 g rump steak, cut into 2 cm cubes
1 onion, chopped
1 clove garlic, crushed
1 x 425 g can tomatoes, drained
2 tablespoons soy sauce
½ teaspoon finely chopped fresh ginger
½ cup beef stock

1 green capsicum, cut into short strips
1 tablespoon cornflour mixed with 2 tablespoons water

1 To prepare sauce: heat oil in a wok or frying pan. Brown meat a little at a time and transfer to a bowl. Add onion and garlic to pan,

Oriental Beef and Noodles (top) and Stir-fried Chicken (bottom)

stirring well for 1–2 minutes.

2 Add drained tomatoes and cook for 5 minutes, pressing tomatoes down with the back of a spoon. Return meat to pan. Stir in soy sauce, ginger and stock. Cover and simmer about 20 minutes or until meat is tender.

3 Add capsicum and cook for another 5 minutes. Add cornflour mixture to pan and boil, stirring for another minute.

4 To prepare pasta: bring a large pan of water and the oil to the boil. Add fettuccine and cook for 6–8 minutes, or until firm and tender. Drain, rinse under warm water and drain again. Place on a warm serving platter and spoon over meat sauce.

HINT
To remove papery coating from a clove of garlic: crush the clove under the flat side of the blade of a cook's knife. Peel away papery coating.

Stir-fried Chicken

Preparation time: 25 minutes
Cooking time: 20 minutes
Serves 4
EASY

1 tablespoon vegetable oil
325 g Chinese noodles

Chicken and Vegetables
2 tablespoons vegetable oil
500 g boned skinned chicken, cut into 1 cm strips
2 thin slices peeled fresh ginger
dash bottled hot chilli sauce
4 cups prepared fresh mixed vegetables (e.g. carrots, tomatoes, broccoli, beans, snow peas or cabbage)
1 cup chicken stock
4 shallots, cut in 5 cm pieces
2 tablespoons soy sauce
2 tablespoons dry sherry or dry vermouth
1½ tablespoons cornflour
1 x 230 g can water chestnuts, drained

1 To prepare pasta: bring a large pan of water and the oil to the boil. Add noodles and cook in boiling water for 3–5 minutes, or until firm and tender. Drain, rinse under warm water and drain again. Keep warm.

2 To prepare chicken and vegetables: heat oil in a wok or large frying pan until hot. Add chicken, ginger and chilli sauce to taste. Stir-fry until chicken turns white. Transfer with a slotted spoon to a bowl. Discard ginger.

3 Add vegetables to wok and stir-fry for 3 minutes. Add stock and cook 3 minutes. Return chicken to wok. Reduce heat and cover. Cook 3 minutes more.

4 Add shallots and cook for 1 minute until tender-crisp. Combine soy sauce, sherry and cornflour. Stir into wok with water chestnuts. Cook, stirring, until thickened, clear and boiling.

5 Spoon chicken mixture over hot noodles in a serving bowl. Toss well and serve at once.

HINT
Store fresh ginger in a pot containing moist sand. Slice off what you require and return remainder to sand. This keeps the ginger fresh and moist.

Spaghetti and Meatballs

Preparation time: 25
  minutes
Cooking time: 50
  minutes
Serves 6
MEDIUM

4 tablespoons oil
500 g spaghetti
grated parmesan cheese
  to serve

Sauce
1 tablespoon oil
1 small onion, chopped
1 x 425 g can tomatoes
4 tablespoons tomato
  paste
½ cup water
½ cup dry red wine
1 small clove garlic,
  crushed
1 bay leaf
pinch black pepper

Meatballs
½ cup milk
1 cup soft breadcrumbs
500g minced steak
1 small onion, very
  finely chopped
1 tablespoon grated
  parmesan cheese
1 egg, beaten
1 tablespoon chopped
  fresh parsley
pinch black pepper
¼ teaspoon dried
  oregano leaves

Spaghetti and Meatballs

18

1 To prepare sauce: heat oil in a pan. Add onion and fry until soft. Add remaining sauce ingredients and simmer for 20 minutes until thick, stirring occasionally.

2 To prepare meatballs: add milk to breadcrumbs and leave for 5 minutes. Combine soaked breadcrumbs with remaining meatball ingredients, mixing lightly but thoroughly. Form into balls and brown on all sides in 3 tablespoons hot oil. Add to sauce and simmer gently for about 15 minutes. Remove bay leaf.

3 To prepare pasta: bring a large pan of water and remaining 1 tablespoon of oil to the boil. Add spaghetti and cook for 10–12 minutes, or until firm and tender. Drain, rinse under warm water and drain again. Spoon meatballs and sauce over spaghetti and serve with grated parmesan cheese.

HINT
You can make soft breadcrumbs by processing bread slices in a food processor until crumbs form. Alternatively, grate stale bread on a fine wire cake rack.

Chilli Pork and Penne

Chilli Pork and Penne

Preparation time: 15 minutes
Cooking time: 35 minutes
Serves 4
EASY

1 tablespoon oil
350 g penne macaroni
parmesan cheese to serve

Sauce
150 g belly pork, cut into strips
1 onion, chopped
2 cloves garlic, crushed
½ fresh or dried chilli, or ½ teaspoon cayenne pepper
1 x 425 g can tomatoes, chopped

1 To prepare sauce: in a pan fry pork in its own fat until cooked through. Drain off excess fat. Add onion and garlic. Remove seeds from chilli and chop flesh finely. Add chilli and chopped tomatoes to pan. Simmer, uncovered, for 15–20 minutes.

2 To prepare pasta: bring a large pan of water and the oil to the boil. Add penne and cook for 10–12 minutes, or until firm and tender. Drain, rinse under warm water and drain again.

3 Place pasta on a warmed serving dish, top with sauce and a light sprinkling of parmesan cheese.

19

Beef and Macaroni (left) and Pasta and Quick Meat Sauce (right)

Beef and Macaroni

Preparation time: 25
  minutes
Cooking time: 1½ hours
Serves 6
EASY

2 *tablespoons oil*
750 g *round or topside
  steak, cut into 2 cm
  cubes*
2 *onions, sliced*
1 *clove garlic, crushed*
¾ *cup beef stock*
2 *sprigs fresh parsley*
1 *bay leaf*
1 *sprig thyme*
1 *cup tomato purée or
  juice*
pinch black pepper

2 *carrots, sliced*
250 g *rigati macaroni*
*chopped fresh parsley to
  garnish*

1 Heat oil in a large
pan. Add meat, onions
and garlic, and fry until
meat browns. Pour off
excess oil from pan.
2 Add ¼ cup beef stock
with the herbs tied
together in a small
bunch. Cover and cook
gently for 30 minutes.
Add half the remaining
stock with the purée,
pepper to taste and
carrots. Stir well.
3 Cover pan and
simmer for another 30
minutes. Stir in the last

of the stock and bring to
boiling point. Mix in
pasta. Bring to the boil
again, cover and cook
10 minutes.
4 Remove lid and
continue cooking until
pasta is quite tender.
Remove herb bunch.
Spoon beef and
macaroni onto a serving
dish and sprinkle with
chopped parsley.

HINT
Partially frozen meat
is much easier to cut
into cubes or slices
than defrosted or
freshly sliced meat.

Pasta and Quick Meat Sauce

Preparation time: 15 minutes
Cooking time: 45 minutes
Serves 4
EASY

1 tablespoon oil
375 g spaghetti
grated parmesan cheese

Sauce
1 tablespoon oil
1 small onion, grated
1 clove garlic, crushed
500 g minced steak
½ teaspoon chopped fresh oregano leaves or ¼ teaspoon dried
1 x 37 g packet spaghetti sauce mix
1 ¾ cups water
1 x 140 g can tomato paste
pinch pepper

1 To prepare sauce: heat oil in a pan. Add onion, garlic and meat. Brown well over high heat, breaking up with the back of a spoon. Add oregano, sauce mix, water, tomato paste and pepper to taste. Bring to the boil, cover and simmer for 15 minutes. Uncover and simmer for another 8–10 minutes.
2 To prepare pasta: bring a large pan of water and the oil to the boil. Add spaghetti and cook for 10–12 minutes, or until firm and tender. Drain, rinse under warm water and drain again.
3 Place spaghetti on a warm serving plate. Spoon sauce over and top with parmesan cheese.

Beef Hotpot

Preparation time: 15 minutes
Cooking time: 1 hour and 10 minutes
Serves 6
EASY

30 g butter
650 g lean beef mince
1 small onion, finely chopped
1 x 440 g can peeled tomatoes, chopped
2 stalks celery, sliced
200 g mushrooms, sliced
2 tablespoons tomato paste
3 teaspoons fresh oregano or basil leaves or 1 teaspoon dried
pinch black pepper

1 ½ cups water
1 small green capsicum, seeded and cut into short, wide strips
1 small red capsicum, seeded and cut into short, wide strips
500 g penne macaroni
4 tablespoons grated parmesan cheese

1 In a large frying pan, melt butter and brown mince and onion. Add tomatoes with liquid, celery, mushrooms, tomato paste, oregano and pepper to taste. Cover and cook over low heat for 20 minutes.
2 Stir in water, capsicums and macaroni; heat to boiling. Turn mixture into an 8-cup baking dish and sprinkle with cheese. Cover and bake at 180°C for 40 minutes or until macaroni and meat are tender.

Beef Hotpot

Burmese Noodles

Burmese Noodles

Preparation time: 30
  minutes
Cooking time: 20
  minutes
Serves 4
EASY

*325 g Chinese egg
  noodles*

*1 double chicken breast,
  boned and skin
  removed*
3 tablespoons oil
3 onions, sliced
3 cloves garlic, crushed
2 tablespoons soy sauce
*1 stalk celery, thinly
  sliced*
*2 cups shredded white
  Chinese cabbage*

*500 g prawns, shelled
  and deveined*
pinch black pepper

1 Pour boiling water
over the noodles and
leave for 10 minutes.
Drop noodles into a
saucepan of boiling
water and cook for
about 3 minutes until

firm and tender. Drain, spread over two thicknesses of absorbent paper on a wire cake cooler and set aside.

2 Cut chicken flesh into short strips. Heat oil in a wok or frying pan. Add onions and garlic, and fry until onions soften. Add chicken strips and fry, stirring for 2–3 minutes. Stir in soy sauce. Cover and cook gently until chicken is tender. Mix in celery and cabbage and cook another 3–4 minutes.

3 Add prawns and pepper to taste and cook for about 2 minutes, until prawns are cooked through. Remove all from pan and set aside to keep hot. Add noodles to pan and toss gently for about 3 minutes. Remove to a warm serving platter and spoon the chicken mixture over the top.

HINTS
☐ Bean sprouts, snow peas and diced ham are great additions to Burmese noodles.

☐ Sometimes this dish is garnished with scrambled eggs. When ready to serve, scramble 2–3 eggs in the same pan until firm, cut into strips and scatter over the top.

Spicy Pasta

Preparation time: 20 minutes
Cooking time: 20 minutes
Serves 6
EASY

1 tablespoon oil
500 g penne macaroni
grated parmesan cheese
   to serve (optional)

Sauce
1 tablespoon oil
1 large onion, sliced
1 clove garlic, crushed
2 cups sliced cabanossi
   (about 2 sticks)
4 mushrooms, sliced
1 x 400 g can artichokes,
   drained and halved
1 x 425 g can tomatoes,
   chopped
10 black olives, sliced
2 teaspoons chopped
   fresh chilli
½ teaspoon dried basil
   leaves
pinch black pepper

1 To prepare pasta: bring large pan of water and a tablespoon of oil to the boil. Add pasta and cook in boiling water for 10–12 minutes, or until firm and tender. Drain, rinse under warm water and drain again. Keep warm.

2 To prepare sauce: heat oil in a large frying pan. Sauté onion and garlic until onion softens. Add cabanossi and mushrooms. Cook for 5 minutes. Stir in remaining ingredients. Simmer gently until heated through. Add a little water or red wine if mixture becomes dry.

3 Place pasta on a serving platter. Pour over sauce. Toss to combine. Serve with salad and crusty bread. Sprinkle pasta with a little parmesan cheese if desired.

Spicy Pasta

Chicken Balls in Tomato Sauce

Preparation time: 30
  minutes
Cooking time: 45
  minutes
Serves 6
MEDIUM

5 tablespoons oil
500 g elbow macaroni

Chicken Balls
500 g chicken mince
2 onions, chopped
¼ teaspoon each dried
  oregano leaves and
  thyme
3 tablespoons dry
  breadcrumbs
1 egg, beaten

Sauce
1 onion, chopped
2 tomatoes, peeled and
  chopped
1 cup tomato purée
1 cup water
1 chicken stock cube
1 tablespoon red wine
  vinegar
1 teaspoon brown sugar
½ teaspoon chilli
  powder
pinch black pepper
2 teaspoons cornflour
  blended with
  1 tablespoon cold
  water

1 To prepare chicken
balls: combine all
ingredients in a bowl.
Mix well. Roll into
walnut-sized balls
between wet hands.
2 Heat 3 tablespoons oil
in a large frying pan.
Add balls a few at a
time. Fry until golden.
Drain on absorbent
paper. Continue with
remaining chicken balls.
Set aside.
3 To prepare sauce: fry
onion in 1 tablespoon oil
until soft. Add
remaining ingredients
except cornflour
mixture. Simmer for 10
minutes. Stir cornflour
mixture into sauce.
Bring to the boil, stirring
constantly. Simmer for 3
minutes.
4 To prepare pasta:
bring a large pan of
water and 1 tablespoon
oil to the boil. Add pasta
and cook for 10
minutes, or until firm
and tender. Drain, rinse
under warm water and
drain again. Spoon
meatballs and sauce over
pasta and serve
immediately.

HINT
Meatballs can be
successfully grilled or
baked in the oven,
rather than fried.

24

Chicken Balls in Tomato Sauce

–FABULOUS SEAFOOD PASTA–

Almost Instant Tagliatelle

*C*aviar, anchovies, fresh and canned fish, and seafood can all combine with many other flavours to produce exotic, delicious sauces, suitable to serve over a bowl of steaming hot pasta.

A sprinkling of fresh herbs and black pepper is often the best topping, since parmesan cheese doesn't usually lend itself to fishy pasta dishes.

Avoid long cooking of fish or seafood, as it becomes tough and very dry. It should only be just cooked, and served immediately.

Almost Instant Tagliatelle

Preparation time: 5 minutes
Cooking time: 8 minutes
Serves 4
EASY

1 tablespoon oil
350 g green tagliatelle noodles
1 x 185 g can tuna in brine, drained and flaked
90 g melted butter
4 tablespoons chopped fresh parsley
1 tablespoon chopped fresh mixed herbs or 1 teaspoon dried
2 cloves garlic, crushed
pinch black pepper

1 To prepare pasta: bring a large pan of water and the oil to the boil. Add tagliatelle and cook for 6–8 minutes, or until firm and tender. Drain, rinse under warm water and drain again.
2 Add remaining ingredients and toss through. Serve immediately in a heated dish.

Tagliatelle with Caviar

Preparation time: 10 minutes
Cooking time: 8 minutes
Serves 6
EASY

1 tablespoon oil
500 g green or white tagliatelle
90 g butter
pinch black pepper
1 x 300 mL carton sour cream
50 g black caviar
50 g red caviar

1 To prepare pasta: bring a large pan of water and the oil to the boil. Add tagliatelle and cook for 6–8 minutes, or until firm and tender. Drain, rinse under warm water and drain again. Add butter and pepper. Toss well.
2 To serve: arrange a portion of pasta on each plate. Top generously with sour cream and caviar.

Tagliatelle with Caviar

Pasta with Mussels

Preparation time: 25 minutes
Cooking time: 30 minutes
Serves 4
MEDIUM

1 tablespoon oil
350 g bow-tie or shell-shaped macaroni
1 tablespoon sour cream (optional)
squeeze of lemon juice
crusty bread to serve
Sauce
1 kg fresh mussels in the shell
1 large brown onion, chopped
¾ cup dry red wine
2 tablespoons olive oil
30 g butter
125 g button mushrooms, sliced
2–3 cloves garlic, crushed
2 x 425 g cans tomatoes, chopped
1 tablespoon tomato paste
2 tablespoons chopped fresh basil leaves or 2 teaspoons dried
2 tablespoons chopped fresh parsley
1 bay leaf, crushed
pinch pepper

1 Pull off hairy beards from mussels.

2 Simmer mussels, half the onion and the wine for 5 minutes.

3 Add undrained tomatoes to mixture and simmer until thickened to a sauce.

4 Combine cooked pasta with sauce and reserved mussels, and heat through.

1 Pull off the hairy beards from mussels and scrub shells well with a stiff brush under cold water to completely remove grit. Discard any mussels that have open shells or those which do not close when sharply tapped.

2 To prepare sauce: in a large saucepan, place mussels, half the onion and the wine. Heat until boiling. Reduce heat, cover and simmer for about 5 minutes until mussels open. Strain, reserving liquid. Discard any unopened shells. Set mussels and liquid aside.

3 In the same pan, heat oil and butter over moderate heat. Add remaining onion with the mushrooms and garlic. Cover and cook gently until onion softens. Add undrained tomatoes, reserved mussel liquid, tomato paste, basil, parsley, bay leaf and pepper to taste. Simmer, uncovered, stirring occasionally until thickened to a sauce.

4 To prepare pasta: bring a large pan of water and the oil to the boil. Add macaroni and cook for 8–10 minutes, or until firm and tender. Drain, rinse under warm water and drain again. Return to pan. Stir in thickened sauce and reserved mussels and heat through. Just before serving, stir in sour cream (if using) and lemon juice to taste. Serve with crusty bread.

5 *Serve Pasta with Mussels piping hot.*

Sicilian Spaghetti and Pasta Marinara

Sicilian Spaghetti

Preparation time: 10
minutes
Cooking time: 17
minutes
Serves 4
EASY

1 tablespoon oil
500 g spaghetti
3 tablespoons chopped
fresh parsley
grated parmesan cheese
to serve

Sauce
1 x 45 g can anchovy
fillets
2 tablespoons olive oil
2 cloves garlic, crushed
2 tablespoons fine dry
breadcrumbs
pinch black pepper

1 To prepare pasta:
bring a large pan of
water and the oil to the
boil. Add spaghetti and
cook for 10–12 minutes,
or until firm and tender.
Drain, rinse under warm
water and drain again.
Place in a warm serving
dish.
2 To prepare sauce:
drain anchovy fillets and
chop. Heat oil in a pan
and fry garlic until soft.
Add anchovies and
cook, stirring, for 2
minutes. Stir in
breadcrumbs and
pepper, and reheat.
3 Spoon sauce over
spaghetti and toss
lightly. Sprinkle with
plenty of chopped
parsley and serve grated

parmesan cheese
separately.

Pasta Marinara

Preparation time: 15
minutes
Cooking time: 35
minutes
Serves 4
EASY

1 tablespoon oil
350 g spaghetti

Sauce
1 tablespoon oil
2 onions, very finely
chopped
2 cloves garlic, crushed

1 x 425 g can tomato
  purée
1 small carrot, coarsely
  grated
3 tablespoons chopped
  celery
1 cup red wine
1 teaspoon chopped
  fresh basil leaves or ½
  teaspoon dried
pinch black pepper
1½ cups mixed
  uncooked seafood
  (e.g. prawns, mussels,
  scallops or crabmeat)

1 To prepare sauce: heat
oil in a pan. Add onions
and fry gently until soft.
Add garlic and fry
another 1–2 minutes.
Add purée, carrot, celery
and wine. Stir until
boiling, reduce heat and
simmer for 15 minutes.
2 To prepare pasta:
bring a large pan of
water and the oil to the
boil. Add spaghetti and
cook for 10–12 minutes,
or until firm and tender.
Drain, rinse under warm
water and drain again.
Place spaghetti in a
warm serving dish.
3 To assemble: stir
basil, pepper to taste and
seafood through wine
sauce. Reheat 1–2
minutes until seafood is
cooked. Pour sauce over
spaghetti and toss
lightly.

Vermicelli Royale

Preparation time: 10
  minutes
Cooking time: 12
  minutes
Serves 2
EASY

1 tablespoon oil
225 g vermicelli (thin
  wheat spaghetti)

Sauce
1 cup cream
2 tablespoons chopped
  shallots or spring
  onions, white part
  only
pinch each paprika and
  pepper
60 g smoked salmon, cut
  into thin strips

Garnish
2 teaspoons salmon or
  red lumpfish caviar
fresh parsley sprigs

1 To prepare pasta:
bring a large pan of
water and the oil to the
boil. Add vermicelli and
cook for 4–5 minutes, or
until firm and tender.
Drain, rinse under warm
water and drain again.
Keep warm.
2 To prepare sauce: in a
small pan, combine
cream and shallots.
Bring to the boil, reduce
heat and simmer for 5
minutes. Stir in
seasonings to taste.
3 Arrange pasta on
warmed serving plates.
Stir salmon into cream
mixture and spoon over
pasta. Garnish with
caviar and parsley. Serve
immediately.

Vermicelli Royale

31

Macaroni Pizza

Macaroni Pizza

Preparation time: 20
   minutes plus
   30 minutes soaking
   time
Cooking time: 50
   minutes
Serves 6
EASY

1 tablespoon oil
350 g small elbow
   macaroni
2 x 45 g cans anchovies
milk
185 g Swiss cheese slices
2 tomatoes, sliced
2 teaspoons chopped
   fresh basil leaves or
   1 teaspoon dried to
   garnish

Sauce
2 tablespoons oil
1 onion, very finely
   chopped
1 clove garlic, crushed
1 x 425 g can peeled
   tomatoes
1 teaspoon chopped
   fresh basil or ½
   teaspoon dried
1 tablespoon tomato
   paste

1 To prepare pasta:
bring a large pan of
water and the oil to the
boil. Add macaroni and
cook for 8–10 minutes,
or until firm and tender.
Drain, rinse under warm
water and drain again.
Drain anchovies. Soak in
a bowl of milk for 30
minutes then drain.
2 To prepare sauce:
heat oil in a pan. Gently
fry onion until golden.

Add garlic, undrained
chopped tomatoes, basil
and tomato paste. Cover
and simmer, stirring
occasionally, for about
20 minutes. Remove
from heat.
3 Grease a shallow
ovenproof dish about 25
x 28 cm. Spread half the
cooked macaroni over.
Spoon a layer of tomato
sauce over, cover with
rest of cooked macaroni.
Add cheese slices and
arrange anchovies in a
lattice pattern over the
top. Put a slice of
tomato in each lattice
square and sprinkle with
basil.
4 Bake at 190°C for
15–20 minutes, or until
heated through and
cheese has melted.

Bali-style Noodles

*Preparation time: 20
  minutes*
*Cooking time: 20
  minutes*
Serves 6
EASY

4 tablespoons vegetable
  oil
500 g capellini egg
  noodles
2 large onions, thinly
  sliced
2 stalks celery, thinly
  sliced
1 green capsicum, thinly
  sliced
1 red capsicum, thinly
  sliced
1–2 hot chillies, thinly
  sliced
3 tablespoons soy sauce
3 tablespoons dry sherry
  or fish stock
oil for deep-frying
2 large onions, thinly
  sliced (extra)
500 g cooked prawns,
  shelled and deveined
  with tails intact

1 To prepare pasta:
bring a large pan of
water and 1 tablespoon
oil to the boil. Add egg
noodles and cook for
4–5 minutes, or until
firm and tender. Drain,
rinse under warm water
and drain again. Keep
warm.

2 Heat remaining 3
tablespoons oil in a large
frying pan. Add
vegetables and cook,
tossing frequently, until
just tender. Add soy
sauce and dry sherry.
Spoon hot noodles over
and cook, tossing
constantly, until all
ingredients are
combined and heated.
3 Deep-fry the extra
onions in oil until
browned and crisp. Add
prawns and heat
through. Turn noodles
onto a heated platter,
and scatter prawns and
onions over the top.

Bali-style Noodles

—PASTA WITH CREAM AND CHEESE—

Fabulous pasta served with butter and cheese

*T*he delicate flavours of fresh cheese, cream and milk combine deliciously with the stronger flavours of hard cheeses, to form pasta sauces that can be made in double quick time.

Enrich sauces with a little egg yolk or a dob of butter and a few seasonings, and you will produce a meal fit for a king.

Buttered Noodles

Preparation time: 5 minutes
Cooking time: 12 minutes
Serves 6
EASY

1 tablespoon oil
500 g fettuccine
60 g butter
1 cup cream
1 cup grated parmesan cheese
pinch black pepper

1 To prepare pasta: bring a large pan of water and the oil to the boil. Add fettuccine and cook for 6–8 minutes, or until firm and tender. Drain, rinse under warm water and drain again. Place in a warm serving bowl.
2 Melt butter in a pan over low heat. Mix in cream, parmesan and pepper, and heat gently. Pour butter mixture over pasta, toss well and serve at once.

Noodle Bake

Preparation time: 10 minutes
Cooking time: 35 minutes
Serves 6
EASY

2½ cups cooked egg noodles
1 cup cottage cheese
1 cup sour cream
½ cup sliced shallots
2 cups Rich Meat Sauce (see recipe)
snipped fresh chives
¾ cup coarsely grated cheddar cheese

1 Combine noodles, cottage cheese, sour cream and shallots. When thoroughly mixed, spoon into a greased shallow ovenproof dish.
2 Pour the meat sauce over, sprinkle lightly with chives and top with grated cheese. Bake at 180°C for about 35 minutes, or until heated through, and bubbling on top.

> **HINT**
> Fresh cream can be soured with the addition of
> 1 teaspoon vinegar per cup of cream.

Noodle Bake

Clockwise from left: Spaghetti Creole, Blue Cheese Tagliatelle, and Spaghetti Carbonara

Spaghetti Creole

Preparation time: 15
  minutes
Cooking time: 30
  minutes
Serves 6
EASY

1 tablespoon oil
500 g spaghetti

chopped fresh parsley to
  garnish

Sauce
60 g butter
500 g green prawns,
  shelled and deveined
100 mL white wine
1 x 425 g can peeled
  tomatoes, crushed
pinch black pepper

2 teaspoons curry
  powder
1 x 300 mL carton
  cream
2 tablespoons grated
  parmesan cheese

1 To prepare sauce:
melt butter in a frying
pan. Cook prawns until
just pink. Remove

prawns from pan and set aside. Add wine, tomatoes, seasonings, cream and cheese. Simmer for 10 minutes.

2 To prepare pasta: bring a large pan of water and the oil to the boil. Add spaghetti and cook for 10–12 minutes, or until firm and tender. Drain, rinse under warm water and drain again. Return to pan. Add prawn sauce. Toss over low heat for 1–2 minutes. Serve garnished with parsley.

> **HINT**
> Devein green prawns by cutting along the back of the prawn with a sharp knife and removing vein.

Spaghetti Carbonara

Preparation time: 10 minutes
Cooking time: 15 minutes
Serves 6
EASY

1 tablespoon oil
500 g spaghetti
chopped fresh chives or parsley to garnish

Sauce
1 teaspoon butter
4 rashers rindless bacon, chopped
1 x 300 mL carton cream
4 egg yolks

2 tablespoons grated parmesan cheese
seasonings to taste

1 To prepare sauce: heat butter in a pan. Cook bacon until brown. Add cream all at once. Bring to the boil. Reduce heat and simmer for 2 minutes. Remove from heat and stir in egg yolks, cheese and seasonings and set aside.
2 To prepare pasta: bring a large pan of water and the oil to the boil. Add spaghetti and cook for 10–12 minutes, or until firm and tender. Drain, rinse under warm water and drain again.
3 Toss sauce through pasta. Garnish with chives. Serve on a warm serving platter.

Blue Cheese Tagliatelle

Preparation time: 10 minutes
Cooking time: 20 minutes
Serves 6
MEDIUM

1 tablespoon oil
500 g white or green tagliatelle
2–3 tablespoons grated parmesan cheese

chopped fresh parsley to garnish

Sauce
30 g butter
2 zucchini, sliced
1 clove garlic, crushed
100 mL white wine
100 g blue cheese, crumbled
1 x 300 mL carton cream
pinch black pepper

1 To prepare sauce: melt butter in a frying pan. Cook zucchini and garlic until zucchini is tender. Stir in wine, cheese, cream and pepper to taste. Simmer for 10 minutes.
2 To prepare pasta: bring a large pan of water and the oil to the boil. Add tagliatelle and cook for 6–8 minutes, or until firm and tender. Drain, rinse under warm water and drain again.
3 Return pasta to pan. Add sauce. Toss through pasta for a few minutes over low heat. Serve sprinkled with parmesan and parsley.

> **HINT**
> Fresh herbs give a better flavour to sauces, so where possible, use fresh rather than dried. Use three times as much fresh herbs as dried, i.e. 1 teaspoon dried herbs = 3 teaspoons fresh.

Pasta, Eggs and Mushrooms

Pasta, Eggs and Mushrooms

Preparation time: 20
  minutes
Cooking time: 35
  minutes
Serves 4
EASY

1 tablespoon oil
350 g small elbow
  macaroni
1 onion, sliced

Sauce
45 g butter
2 tablespoons plain flour
1½ cups milk

pinch cayenne pepper
4 tablespoons grated
  tasty cheddar cheese
125 g small mushrooms,
  sliced
4 hard-boiled eggs
¾ cup soft breadcrumbs
60 g melted butter

1 To prepare pasta:
bring a large pan of
water and the oil to the
boil. Add macaroni and
onion and cook for 8–10
minutes, or until firm
and tender. Drain, rinse
under warm water and
drain again.
2 To prepare sauce:

melt butter in a pan.
Add flour and stir for
1–2 minutes. Add milk
and cook, stirring, until
boiling. Stir in pepper
and cheese, and simmer
for 1–2 minutes, or until
cheese melts. Quickly fry
the mushrooms in a little
butter until softened.
Mix drained macaroni
into the sauce with the
mushrooms.
3 To assemble: spoon
half the macaroni and
onion into a greased,
shallow ovenproof dish.
Halve the eggs
lengthways and arrange

over the top, cut-side down. Cover with remaining macaroni.
4 Toss breadcrumbs in melted butter until coated. Sprinkle over macaroni. Bake at 190°C for about 15 minutes, or until heated through.

Spinach Gnocchi

Preparation time: 40 minutes
Cooking time: 45 minutes
Serves 4
MEDIUM

Gnocchi are small savoury oval shapes originally called ravioli in Italy. Although they do not truly come under the label pasta, they figure largely on the pasta menus of Italian restaurants in Australia. They are usually made with potato and served with melted butter, grated cheese or sauces such as tomato, cream or chicken liver.

750 g fresh spinach or young silverbeet, cleaned, trimmed and very finely chopped
400 g ricotta cheese

Spinach Gnocchi

2 eggs
1 cup freshly grated parmesan cheese
pinch pepper
pinch ground nutmeg
a little plain flour for rolling
90 g butter, melted

1 Place spinach in a bowl with ricotta, eggs, half the parmesan cheese, pepper and nutmeg to taste. Mix well until blended.
2 With flour-dusted hands, shape spinach mixture into 5 cm balls; lightly coat with a little flour to prevent sticking. Set aside on greaseproof paper until needed.
3 Heat a large pan of water to boiling. Drop gnocchi 3–4 at a time into water. Simmer until they float to the surface. Remove with a slotted spoon and drain briefly.
4 Transfer gnocchi to a buttered shallow baking dish. Top with remaining parmesan cheese and drizzle with melted butter. Bake at 200°C for 15 minutes until browned.

HINT
When cooking gnocchi, ensure water is kept at simmering point only — rapidly boiling water can cause the gnocchi to disintegrate.

Noodle Shell Quiche (left) and Pasta with Broccoli (right)

Noodle Shell Quiche

Preparation time: 25
  minutes
Cooking time: 45
  minutes
Serves 4
EASY

*325 g very thin
  spaghetti, broken into
  pieces*
2 tablespoons oil
*250 g rindless bacon, cut
  into 5 cm pieces*
1 onion, chopped
4 eggs
1⅔ cups milk
*125 g Swiss cheese,
  shredded*
*½ cup grated parmesan
  cheese*
*½ teaspoon dried basil
  leaves*
*¼ teaspoon pepper
generous pinch nutmeg*

1 To prepare pasta:
bring a large pan of
water and 1 tablespoon
of oil to the boil. Add
spaghetti and cook for
6–8 minutes, or until
firm and tender. Drain,
rinse under cold water
and drain again. Place
into the base and sides of
a buttered 25 cm quiche
dish.
2 To assemble: fry
bacon until crisp in
remaining oil; drain and
spoon onto noodle base.
Sauté onion in bacon
dripping for about 3
minutes. Sprinkle over
bacon and pasta. Whisk
eggs and milk together,
stir in cheeses, basil,
pepper and nutmeg to
taste. Pour into dish.
3 Bake at 180°C for
about 30 minutes until
filling is set and shell
begins to brown. Cool
slightly before cutting
into wedges to serve.

Pasta with Broccoli

Preparation time: 15
minutes
Cooking time: 20
minutes
Serves 6
EASY

1 *tablespoon oil*
500 g *spaghetti*
3 *cups broccoli florets*
4 *tablespoons sliced*
shallots
250 g *very small*
tomatoes, halved or
quartered (optional)
3 *tablespoons chopped*
fresh continental
parsley

Sauce
45 g *butter*
1 *tablespoon plain flour*
pinch pepper
¼ *teaspoon dried basil*
leaves
¼ *teaspoon dried*
oregano leaves
1½ *cups milk*
250 g *ricotta cheese*
125 g *mozzarella cheese,*
diced

1 To prepare sauce:
melt butter in a pan.
Add flour and
seasonings, and cook for
2–3 minutes, stirring.
Add milk and stir until
boiling and thickened.
Mix in cheeses, stirring
over low heat until
thoroughly combined.
2 To prepare pasta:
bring a large pan of
water and the oil to the
boil. Add spaghetti and
cook for 10–12 minutes,
or until firm and tender.

Drain, rinse under warm
water and drain again.
Steam broccoli over
boiling spaghetti water
until crisp-tender, about
3–4 minutes.
3 Drain spaghetti and
toss with broccoli,
shallots and tomatoes.
Spoon into a heated
dish. Pour hot sauce
over. Garnish with
parsley. (If sauce is too
thick, thin with milk or
cream.)

Parsley Garlic Noodles

Preparation time: 20
minutes
Cooking time: 8 minutes
Serves 6
EASY

1 *tablespoon oil*
500 g *fettuccine*

Sauce
3 *tablespoons white*
wine
3 *slices thick white*
bread, crusts removed

1 *cup chopped fresh*
parsley
3 *cloves garlic, crushed*
¼ *teaspoon black*
pepper
½ *cup olive oil*

1 To prepare sauce:
sprinkle wine over bread
and soak for 10 minutes,
then break into pieces.
2 Combine parsley,
garlic and pepper and
gradually add olive oil.
Add the bread, a little at
a time, beating after
each addition until
mixture is smooth and
thick. Set aside.
3 To prepare pasta:
bring a large pan of
water and the oil to the
boil. Add fettuccine and
cook for 6–8 minutes, or
until firm and tender.
Drain, rinse under warm
water and drain again.
Transfer pasta to a
warm serving bowl,
spoon sauce over hot
pasta and toss to
combine.

Parsley Garlic Noodles

–PASTA AND VEGETABLES–

Spaghetti Napoletana

Combine the versatility of pasta with the endless variety of vegetables and you have the basis of many delicious meals. The range of interesting combinations here will please the vegetarian and non vegetarian alike.

Spaghetti Napoletana

Preparation time: 20 minutes
Cooking time: 20 minutes
Serves 4
EASY

1 tablespoon oil
500 g spaghetti
grated parmesan or romano cheese to serve

Sauce
2 tablespoons oil
1 onion, sliced
2 cloves garlic, crushed
500 g tomatoes, peeled and coarsely chopped
1 teaspoon sugar
1 bay leaf
pinch black pepper
1 teaspoon chopped fresh basil leaves or ½ teaspoon dried

1 To prepare pasta: bring a large pan of water and the oil to the boil. Add spaghetti and cook for 10–12 minutes, or until firm and tender. Drain, rinse under warm water and drain again. Keep warm.

2 To prepare sauce: heat oil in a pan. Fry onion and garlic gently until softened. Add tomatoes, sugar, bay leaf, and black pepper to taste. Cover and simmer until tomatoes are quite soft. Stir in basil and remove bay leaf.
3 Transfer spaghetti to a warm serving bowl. Pour the sauce over and toss lightly. Serve cheese separately.

Spaghetti with Spinach Sauce

Preparation time: 15 minutes
Cooking time: 20 minutes
Serves 4
EASY

1 tablespoon oil
500 g spaghetti

Sauce
1 tablespoon oil

3 cloves garlic, crushed
2 x 250 g packets frozen spinach, thawed and drained
90 g pine nuts or chopped walnuts
2 teaspoons dried basil leaves
½ cup grated parmesan cheese

1 To prepare pasta: bring a large pan of water and the oil to the boil. Add spaghetti and cook for 10–12 minutes, or until firm and tender. Drain, rinse under warm water and drain again. Keep warm.
2 To prepare sauce: heat oil in a large frying pan. Sauté garlic until softened, stirring regularly. Add spinach, nuts, basil and cheese. Cook for about 5 minutes until thoroughly heated. Spoon sauce over spaghetti and serve.

Spaghetti with Spinach Sauce

Ricotta Lasagne Swirls

Preparation time: 45
  minutes
Cooking time: 1 hour
Serves 6
EASY

*1 tablespoon vegetable
  oil*
*12 fluted-edged or plain
  lasagne noodles*
*500 g fresh spinach,
  washed and chopped
  or 1 x 250 g packet
  frozen spinach,
  thawed and very well
  drained*
1½ cups ricotta cheese
*250 g mozzarella cheese,
  shredded*
*1 large egg, lightly
  beaten*
*2 tablespoons grated
  parmesan cheese*
*¼ teaspoon ground
  nutmeg*
¼ teaspoon pepper
60 g butter
*250 g fresh small
  mushrooms,
  quartered*
*1 x 445 g can or jar
  Italian cooking sauce*
*½ cup red wine, beef or
  chicken stock*
*½ teaspoon dried
  oregano leaves*
*½ teaspoon dried basil
  leaves*
*chopped fresh parsley to
  garnish (optional)*

Ricotta Lasagne Swirls (left) Macaroni Caprese (right)

1 To prepare pasta:
bring a large pan of
water and the oil to the
boil. Add lasagne
noodles and cook for 10
minutes, or until firm
and tender. Drain and
rinse under cold water.
Stand in a bowl of cold
water.
2 Steam fresh spinach
with a little simmering
water in a covered pan
for 5–7 minutes. Drain
well. (If using thawed
frozen spinach, drain
well, squeezing out
excess moisture with the
back of a spoon.) In a
bowl, combine spinach,
ricotta, half the
mozzarella, the egg,
parmesan, nutmeg and
pepper. Set mixture
aside.
3 Melt butter in a pan.
Sauté mushrooms over
high heat until just
wilted. Remove from
heat and cool. Combine
Italian cooking sauce,
wine, oregano and basil.
Spoon half the mixture
into a baking dish. Lift
noodles, one at a time,
from water and drain on
paper towels. Spread
each with 3 tablespoons
of cheese mixture. Place

44

An unusual Italian-style entrée — uncooked sauce is tossed through pasta.

1 tablespoon oil
500 g macaroni
125 g mozzarella cheese, cut into small squares
grated parmesan cheese to serve

Sauce
12 egg tomatoes or 4 large tomatoes, thinly sliced
3 cloves garlic, crushed
1 red capsicum, thinly sliced
1 tablespoon chopped fresh basil leaves
½ cup olive oil
pinch black pepper

1 To prepare sauce: place tomatoes in bowl with garlic, capsicum, basil, olive oil and pepper to taste. Cover and leave at room temperature for 1 hour.
2 To prepare pasta: bring a large pan of water and the oil to the boil. Add macaroni and cook for 8–10 minutes, or until firm and tender. Drain, rinse under warm water and drain again. While pasta is still hot, add mozzarella, then the sauce, and toss together. Serve with a bowl of parmesan cheese to sprinkle on top.

3–4 mushroom quarters along each narrow end and roll up, Swiss-roll fashion, around mushrooms. Place, seam-side down, in prepared dish. Spoon remaining sauce over rolls. Cover dish with foil or a lid.
4 Bake at 180°C for 25 minutes. Remove foil and sprinkle with remaining mozzarella cheese and top centre of dish with any leftover mushrooms. Bake for about 5 minutes more, until cheese melts. Sprinkle top with chopped parsley, if desired, before serving.

Macaroni Caprese

Preparation time: 15 minutes plus 1 hour standing time
Cooking time: 10 minutes
Serves 6
EASY

Pasta Tomato Bocconcini (left) and Spirals with Potato and Spinach (right)

Pasta Tomato Bocconcini

Preparation time: 10 minutes
Cooking time: 10 minutes
Serves 4
EASY

2 tablespoons olive oil
325 g large tube macaroni e.g. rigati or mille righe

Tomato Bocconcini
4 ripe tomatoes, peeled, seeded and cut into chunks
3 balls fresh mozzarella (bocconcini), cut into small cubes
12 black olives
¼ teaspoon dried oregano leaves
1 tablespoon fresh basil leaves or ¼ teaspoon dried
pinch pepper
2 tablespoons olive oil

1 To prepare pasta: bring a large pan of water and 1 tablespoon oil to the boil. Add macaroni and cook for 8–10 minutes, or until firm and tender. Drain, rinse under cold water and drain again. Stir through 1 tablespoon olive oil and cool.

2 To prepare bocconcini: combine tomatoes, mozzarella and olives in a bowl. Add the herbs and pepper to taste. Drizzle with 2 tablespoons oil and lightly toss to combine.

3 Spoon mixture over cold pasta and toss to mix. Serve on chilled plates.

> **HINT**
> Extra virgin olive oil is the best to use as a flavouring oil in pasta dishes. For cooking, it is better to use the less expensive pure olive oil.

Spirals with Potatoes and Spinach

Preparation time: 20 minutes
Cooking time: 25 minutes
Serves 4
EASY

3 tablespoons olive oil
325 g fusilli, trevelle or spiral macaroni

300 g new potatoes, peeled and thickly sliced
1 clove garlic, crushed
2 dried red chillies, finely crushed
½ bunch fresh spinach, trimmed, washed and roughly chopped
pinch pepper

1 To prepare pasta: bring a large pan of water and 1 tablespoon oil to the boil. Add macaroni and cook for 8–10 minutes, or until firm and tender. Drain, rinse under warm water and drain again. Cook potatoes in boiling water until tender. Drain and add to pasta. Place in a warm serving bowl.

2 Heat remaining 2 tablespoons oil in small pan. Add garlic and chillies and sauté for 1–2 minutes until garlic is tender. Add spinach and cook over high heat 2–3 minutes until wilted and tender.

3 Pour over pasta mixture in bowl. Season to taste with pepper and lightly toss.

> **HINT**
> Leave the skin on the potatoes for added fibre and a tasty treat.

Mexican Pasta

Preparation time: 20 minutes
Cooking time: 25 minutes
Serves 6
EASY

20 g butter
1 onion, finely sliced
1 red capsicum, seeded and thickly sliced
3 stalks celery, cut in 2 cm pieces
2 cobs fresh sweet corn, cut in 2 cm pieces
500 g shell macaroni uncooked
1 x 35 g packet taco seasoning mix
2 cups water

1 Melt butter in a large pan. Add onion, capsicum and celery, and sauté for 5 minutes.

2 Add corn pieces, macaroni, seasoning mix and water. Bring to the boil and boil for 15 minutes until macaroni and corn are cooked.

3 Serve hot as an accompaniment to meat or poultry.

> **HINT**
> Purchase corn wrapped in its husk — the husk keeps the corn fresh for longer. Avoid purchasing in plastic wrap, since it makes the corn sweat, therefore losing moisture and drying it out.

–FRESH PASTA SALADS–

Mediterranean Salad (left) and Macaroni Salad (right)

*P*asta is delicious in salads. Combined with soft meats such as chicken or ham, or with crunchy vegetables, pasta's tender yet firm texture adds variety. The following recipes are perfect for summer nights on the verandah or entertaining with a barbecue.

Mediterranean Salad

Preparation time: 20 minutes
Cooking time: 10 minutes
Serves 6
EASY

Salad
3 tablespoons olive oil
500 g penne macaroni
1 small red capsicum, seeded and cut into fine strips
90 g peperoni, skinned and cut into julienne strips
1 tomato, coarsely chopped
1 cup shredded zucchini
¾ cup shredded provolone or cheddar cheese
½ cup chopped fresh parsley
4 tablespoons pitted black olives
4 tablespoons finely chopped onion

Vinaigrette
4–5 tablespoons olive oil
1–2 tablespoons red wine vinegar
1 clove garlic, crushed
2 tablespoons chopped fresh basil leaves or 2 teaspoons dried
1/4 teaspoon dried oregano leaves
pinch black pepper

1 To prepare salad: bring a large pan of water and 1 tablespoon oil to the boil. Add macaroni and cook for 8–10 minutes, or until firm and tender. Drain, rinse under cold water and drain again. Transfer to a large bowl. Add remaining oil and toss well. Add remaining salad ingredients and toss lightly to mix.
2 To prepare vinaigrette: whisk together all ingredients, seasoning to taste. Pour over salad and toss. Cover and chill until served.

HINT
Capsicums are delicious with the skin removed. Cut in half lengthways, remove seeds and place under a hot grill until skin blisters and blackens. Rub off skin.

Macaroni Salad

Preparation time: 15 minutes
Cooking time: 10 minutes
Serves 4
EASY

1 tablespoon oil
325 g small shell macaroni
Italian dressing
1 x 440 g can four bean mix
½ cup sliced stuffed olives
4 stalks celery, sliced
1 white onion, grated
2 tablespoons chopped fresh parsley
mayonnaise (optional)

1 To prepare pasta: bring a large pan of water and the oil to the boil. Add macaroni and cook for 8–10 minutes, or until firm and tender. Drain, rinse under cold water and drain again. Transfer to a bowl, add enough Italian dressing to moisten and toss lightly.
2 Drain beans, rinse in cold water and drain again. Add to pasta with olives, celery and onion. Sprinkle over a little more dressing and toss. Cover and chill. When ready to serve, sprinkle chopped parsley over the top and, if you wish, serve with mayonnaise or Italian dressing.

Garden Pasta Salad with Frankfurters

Preparation time: 15
  minutes
Cooking time: 15
  minutes
Serves 4
EASY

1 *tablespoon oil*
325 *g penne, ziti or*
  spiral macaroni
1 *small bunch fresh*
  asparagus, trimmed
  and cut in 4 cm
  lengths
2–3 *continental*
  frankfurters, sliced
2 *cups mixed cooked*
  vegetables, e.g.
  carrots, green beans,
  peas, or corn
egg mayonnaise
pinch black pepper

1 To prepare pasta:
bring a large pan of
water and the oil to the
boil. Add macaroni and
cook for 8–10 minutes,
or until firm and tender.
Drain, rinse under cold
water and drain again.
2 In a separate large
pan, cook asparagus
with frankfurters in
simmering water until
asparagus is tender-
crisp. Drain well.
3 Combine pasta and
frankfurter mixture in a
serving bowl with
cooked vegetables. Add
mayonnaise and
seasoning to taste; toss
lightly to coat
ingredients. Serve at
room temperature or
lightly chilled, as
desired.

Chicken Pasta Bowl

Preparation time: 20
  minutes
Cooking time: 10
  minutes
Serves 6
EASY

Salad
1 *tablespoon oil*
500 *g macaroni*
3 *cups steamed mixed*
  vegetables
2 *cups diced cooked*
  chicken
200 *g cheddar cheese,*
  diced
2 *stalks celery, sliced*

Dressing
½ *cup oil*
4 *tablespoons tarragon*
  vinegar
½ *teaspoon sugar*
½ *teaspoon dried*
  marjoram leaves
¼ *teaspoon dry mustard*
¼ *teaspoon pepper*
2 *tablespoons chopped*
  fresh parsley
2 *tablespoons chopped*
  shallots

1 To prepare salad:
bring a large pan of
water and the oil to the
boil. Add macaroni and
cook for 8–10 minutes,
or until firm and tender.
Drain, rinse under cold
water and drain again.
Cool. Transfer to a
serving bowl and
combine with
vegetables, chicken,
cheese and celery.
2 To prepare dressing:
combine ingredients in a
jar with a tightfitting lid
and shake vigorously
until blended. Pour
dressing over macaroni
mixture and toss well.
Chill several hours
before serving.

Ham and Pasta Salad

Preparation time: 15
  minutes plus
  overnight chilling time
Cooking time: 10
  minutes
Serves 6
EASY

Dressing
¾ *cup olive oil*
3 *tablespoons red wine*
  vinegar
1½ *tablespoons lemon*
  juice
2 *tablespoons chopped*
  fresh basil leaves or
  1–2 teaspoons dried
½ *teaspoon pepper*

Salad
1 *tablespoon oil*
500 *g ziti or penne*
  macaroni
375 *g zucchini, cut into*
  short julienne strips
250 *g carrots, cut into*
  short julienne strips
185 *g cooked ham, cut*
  into 1 cm cubes

1 To prepare dressing:
in a blender container
combine all ingredients,

cover and blend until smooth. Set aside.

2 To prepare salad: bring a large pan of water and the oil to the boil. Add macaroni and cook for 8–10 minutes, or until firm and tender. Drain, rinse under cold water and drain again.

3 Pour dressing over warm macaroni and gently toss to coat. Cool. Transfer to a serving dish, cover and chill overnight to blend flavours (stir once or twice).

4 Next day, partially cook zucchini and carrots in a little boiling water for 2 minutes until crispy tender. Drain, rinse in cold running water until cold. Drain well.

5 To serve: stir vegetables and ham through macaroni and toss to mix.

Chicken Pasta Bowl (left) and Ham and Pasta Salad (right)

51

—DESSERT PASTAS—

Flambéed Bows in Orange Liqueur Cream Sauce

*T*raditionally pasta is considered a food served as a savoury dish, but this needn't always be the case. Here is a selection of sweet pastas boiled, baked or fried, to tempt the fussiest taste buds.

Where possible, avoid serving a pasta dessert after a pasta meal, as it is much too heavy. Pasta desserts make a grand finale to a meal that is light and simple.

Flambéed Bows in Orange Liqueur Cream Sauce

Preparation time: 15 minutes
Cooking time: 10 minutes
Serves 6
MEDIUM

1 tablespoon oil
500 g fresh pasta bows or twists
1 orange
1 lemon
125 g butter
½ cup sugar
2 tablespoons custard powder
1 cup milk
3 tablespoons cream
3 tablespoons Irish cream
3 tablespoons orange liqueur
vanilla ice-cream to serve

1 To prepare pasta: bring a large pan of water and the oil to the boil. Add bows and cook for 2–3 minutes, or until firm and tender. Drain, rinse under cold water and drain again.
2 To prepare sauce: grate orange and lemon zest. Finely squeeze juice and strain. Set aside. Melt butter in a large chafing dish, add sugar and citrus zest. Cook over low heat for 2–3 minutes. Stir in juice and bring to the boil. Blend custard powder, milk and cream together until smooth. Stir into orange sauce and return to the boil. Stir through pasta shapes and Irish cream.
3 Pour in orange liqueur, warm lightly and ignite. Serve warm with a scoop of vanilla ice-cream.

Spiced Risone Pudding

Preparation time: 15 minutes
Cooking time: 50 minutes
Serves 6
EASY

125 g risone (see Note)
1½ cups milk
1 cup cream

4 tablespoons sugar
10 cm strip orange zest
1 cinnamon stick
½ teaspoon cardamom seeds
20 g butter
3 eggs, separated
½ cup caster sugar
2 teaspoons orange flower water
ice-cream or cream to serve

1 Place risone in a pan with milk, cream, sugar, zest, cinnamon and cardamom. Bring to the boil and simmer for 20–25 minutes until risone is tender and milk absorbed. Remove from heat, stir through butter and cool slightly.
2 Grease a shallow ovenproof dish. When mixture is cool, remove cinnamon stick and orange zest. Stir through egg yolks. Pour into dish and bake at 180°C for 20 minutes.
3 Beat egg whites until stiff. Gradually beat in sugar, a tablespoon at a time. Lastly beat in orange flower water. Pile egg white mixture on risone mixture. Return to oven and continue baking 5–10 minutes until meringue is golden and set. Serve warm with ice-cream or cream.
Note: risone is pasta that resembles rice in appearance. Available from delicatessens or large supermarkets.

Apple Cream Lasagne (below) Spiced Risone Pudding (above) (recipe on p. 53)

Apple Cream Lasagne

Preparation time: 40 minutes
Cooking time: 40 minutes
Serves 12
EASY

240 g instant lasagne noodles
vanilla ice-cream to serve

Apple Layer
1 x 740 g can pie apple
3 tablespoons brown sugar
2 teaspoons ground cinnamon
100 g pecans, roughly chopped

Cream Layer
250 g cream cheese, softened
3 tablespoons brown sugar
3 eggs

300 mL carton fresh cream
2 teaspoons vanilla essence

Crumble Topping
60 g butter
8 slices wholemeal bread, crumbed
½ cup sugar

1   Place lasagne noodles in a large bowl. Cover with warm water and

soak for 10 minutes. Drain.

2 To prepare apple layer: combine pie apple with brown sugar and cinnamon, mixing well to break up apple into small pieces. Stir through pecans. Set aside.

3 To make cream layer: beat cream cheese with sugar until light and fluffy. Beat in eggs, cream and vanilla essence or purée all ingredients in a food processor. Set aside.

4 To make crumble topping: melt butter in a frypan. Stir through breadcrumbs and cook for 2–3 minutes until browned and crispy. Add sugar and cook a further minute. Cool mixture.

5 To assemble: grease a shallow lasagne dish well with butter. Spoon half the apple mixture into the base and cover with a sheet of lasagne. Spread over half the cream mixture, top with a second lasagne sheet. Sprinkle over half the crumbs and again top with a sheet of lasagne. Repeat apple and cream layers and sprinkle remaining crumbs directly onto cream layer. Bake at 180°C for 35–40 minutes or until browned and golden. Stand 15 minutes before serving. Serve warm with vanilla ice-cream.

Tropical Dip with Pasta Triangles

Preparation time: 25 minutes
Cooking time: 10 minutes
Serves 8
EASY

1 quantity fresh Almond Pasta dough (see recipe)
oil for deep-frying
sifted icing sugar for sprinkling

Dip
300 mL sour cream
pulp of 2 passionfruit
1 x 440 g can crushed pineapple, drained
200 g white marshmallows, chopped
1 cup shredded coconut

1 To prepare dip: combine sour cream, passionfruit, pineapple, marshmallows and coconut. Spoon into a small serving bowl and refrigerate for 1 hour.

2 To prepare pasta: follow recipe directions and roll out pasta on a lightly floured board (or through a pasta machine to the second thinnest setting). Cut pasta into 8 cm squares and cut each square diagonally across to form a triangle. Heat oil to 190°C.

3 Deep-fry triangles a few at a time until golden and crispy. Drain on absorbent paper. Sprinkle liberally with icing sugar. Serve dip surrounded by fried pasta.

Tropical Dip with Pasta Triangles

Pasta Stuffed with Spicy Nut Filling

Preparation time: 20 minutes
Cooking time: 45 minutes
Makes 15 filled shells
EASY

250 g large shell pasta
Crème à l'Anglaise to serve (see recipe)

Filling
125 g ground walnuts or pecans
125 g ground almonds
1½ cups cake crumbs
2 tablespoons sugar
¼ teaspoon ground cinnamon
¼ teaspoon ground nutmeg
½ teaspoon ground ginger
lightly beaten egg white to moisten
oil for deep-frying

1 To prepare pasta: bring a large pan of water to the boil. Add pasta shells and cook for 12–15 minutes, or until firm and tender. Drain, rinse under cold running water and drain thoroughly.
2 To prepare filling: combine walnuts, almonds, cake crumbs, sugar, cinnamon, nutmeg and ginger. Moisten with egg white until mixture is just holding together.
3 To assemble: take approximately 2 teaspoons of nut mixture and mould into each pasta shell. Press 2 filled shells together. Stand on a flat tray and chill, uncovered, for 30 minutes.
4 Heat oil to 190°C. Fry shells a few at a time for 3–5 minutes or until golden and crispy. Drain on absorbent paper and serve warm, with a little Crème à l'Anglaise.
Variation:
Dip cooled shells in melted chocolate to serve as petits fours.

Pasta Stuffed with Spicy Nut Filling

Crème à l'Anglaise

Preparation time: 10 minutes
Cooking time: 10 minutes
Makes 1¾ cups

½ cup cream
¾ cup milk
3 egg yolks
2 tablespoons sugar
3 teaspoons cornflour
2 tablespoons orange flavoured liqueur

1 Place cream and ½ cup milk in a pan and bring to boil. Remove from heat.

2 Beat together egg yolks, sugar, cornflour and remaining ¼ cup milk until pale and blended. Pour a little hot milk into egg mixture and combine. Add mixture to pan and blend.

3 Stir over moderate heat until mixture boils and thickens. Remove from heat and stir in liqueur. Cover with wet greaseproof paper until ready to serve.

Almond Tortellini with Fresh Fruit and Mascarpone

Preparation time: 45
    minutes
Cooking time: 20
    minutes
Serves 8
MEDIUM

*500 g fresh mascarpone
    cheese*
300 mL sour cream
1 cup honey
*1 x 250 g punnet
    strawberries, washed
    and hulled*
*4 kiwi fruit, peeled and
    quartered*
*1 quantity fresh Almond
    Pasta dough (see recipe)*
1 egg white
60 g sugar
*2 cups desiccated
    coconut*
oil for deep-frying

1 Mix mascarpone with sour cream and beat thoroughly to combine. Divide between six individual serving dishes and drizzle over 2 tablespoons honey. Arrange fruit on individual serving plates and refrigerate until chilled.

2 To prepare pasta: follow recipe directions and roll pasta out thinly. Cut into 10 cm rounds. Cover with a lightly dampened cloth and set aside. Whisk egg white until stiff. Beat in sugar a little at a time, until shiny and glossy. Fold in coconut and combine. Spoon 2 teaspoons of mixture on each round of pasta. Brush half the edge with a little water. Fold in half and press edges together to seal. Heat oil to 190°C. Deep-fry a few at a time for 3–5 minutes until golden and crisp. Drain on absorbent paper. Serve warm on individual plates with fresh fruit and mascarpone.

Almond Tortellini with Fresh Fruit and Mascarpone

–PERFECT ACCOMPANIMENTS–

Clockwise from top left: a typical Antipasto Platter (all of the ingredients shown are available from delicatessens), Italian Style Salad and Italian Bread,

*T*his chapter contains recipes for entrées, accompaniments and sweets, none of which contains pasta in their ingredients. They have been chosen from predominantly Italian dishes, because they go so well with pasta, complementing flavours and textures perfectly.

The addition of one of these to your pasta main course will help you to compose a perfect Italian meal.

The Antipasto Platter

Antipasto is the selection of hors d'oeuvres served at the beginning of the meal. The antipasto platter can be as simple or as elaborate as you wish to make it.

Italian delicatessens have a range of foods suitable to include on the antipasto platter with little or no preparation. These include:

slices of salami sausage
olives
anchovies
ham
artichokes in oil
mushrooms or funghi in oil or vinegar
pimientos in oil
antipasto vegetables
thin slices of cheese
sun-dried tomatoes

Figs and melon are also welcome additions and blend beautifully with thin slices of prosciutto or Parma ham, which is a raw salted ham served in paper-thin slices.

Other no-fuss additions include lightly fried eggplant, chunks of cucumber, cubed cooked potatoes, sliced raw onion, slices of fennel, radishes and hard-boiled eggs.

Fresh seafood served in olive oil and vinegar or with mayonnaise is also very popular and easy to prepare.

Arrange the platter so that you get an attractive contrast of colours and shapes.

Italian Style Salad

Preparation time: 10 minutes
Cooking time: nil
Serves 8
EASY

Salad
¼ *bunch endive*
1 *cos lettuce*
1 *radicchio or coral lettuce*
1 *fennel bulb, thinly sliced*

1 x 250 g *punnet cherry tomatoes, washed*
1 *red onion, thinly sliced*
1 *red capsicum, finely sliced*
¼ *telegraph cucumber, washed and thickly sliced*

Italian Dressing
4 *tablespoons lemon juice*
4 *tablespoons olive oil*
1 *clove garlic, crushed*
1 *teaspoon finely chopped fresh oregano leaves*
½ *teaspoon finely grated lemon zest*
1 *tablespoon parmesan cheese*
¼ *teaspoon black pepper*

1 Wash lettuce, endive and radicchio thoroughly. Separate leaves and arrange on a large shallow platter. Arrange fennel, tomatoes, onion, capsicum and cucumber on top of salad leaves.
2 To make dressing: combine all ingredients in a small bowl and whisk to combine.

HINT
Use any of the lovely salad greens in season to make this salad, including cos lettuce, butter lettuce, coral lettuce, sorrel and spinach.

Fresh Pears Poached in White Wine (left) and Zabaglione (right)

Fresh Pears Poached in White Wine

Preparation time: 15
   minutes
Cooking time: 20
   minutes
Serves 4
EASY

4 *ripe pears*
2 *cups water*
1 *cup white wine*
1 *cup sugar*
1 *cinnamon stick*
1 *strip lemon rind*

1 Peel pears leaving
stalk attached. Remove
core section with an
apple corer, leaving
pears intact.
2 Place water, wine,
sugar, cinnamon stick
and lemon rind in a large
pan. Bring to the boil.

Add pears and poach
gently for 5–10 minutes,
depending on ripeness of
pears. Pears should be
firm but tender when
tested with a skewer.
Lift pears out of liquid
with a slotted spoon. Set
aside.
3 Boil syrup rapidly for
5–10 minutes or until
slightly thickened.
Spoon over pears and
serve warm or chilled.

Zabaglione

Preparation time: 10
    minutes
Cooking time: 5 minutes
Serves 4
MEDIUM

6 egg yolks
2 tablespoons caster
    sugar
1 cup marsala
sponge fingers to serve

1 Place egg yolks and
sugar in a heat-proof
bowl. Whisk together
until pale and creamy.
Stir in the marsala.
2 Cook mixture over a
pan of simmering water,
whisking constantly
with a balloon whisk or
an electric hand beater.
When mixture is thick
and frothy, pour
immediately into
individual glasses and
serve with a sponge
finger.
Note: it is important to
make zabaglione just
before serving, since the
cooked mixture
separates and becomes
runny soon after
cooking.

HINT
A beaten egg white
folded lightly through
the cooked
zabaglione makes it a
little less rich and
lighter in texture.

Lemon Water Ice

Preparation time: 20
    minutes plus freezing
    time
Cooking time: 5 minutes
Serves 6
EASY

This refreshing water ice
is characteristically icy in
texture, and makes the
ideal finish to a rich
meal.

600 mL water
⅔ cup crystal sugar
300 mL freshly squeezed
    lemon juice

1 Place water and sugar
in a pan and bring to the
boil over moderate heat.
Boil rapidly for 5
minutes. Remove from
heat and cool to room
temperature. Stir
through lemon juice and
place in the refrigerator
until chilled.
2 Transfer mixture to a
shallow metal tray and
place in the coldest part
of the freezer. Stir
mixture every 30
minutes until mixture is
frozen firm. Transfer to
a large container, cover
and store in the freezer
until needed.
3 To serve: spoon a
little lemon ice into
chilled glasses.

HINT
Scoop flesh out of
lemon halves after
juicing and fill lemon
shells with water ice.
Cover and store in the
freezer.

Lemon Water Ice

Italian Bread

Preparation time: 10
  minutes
Cooking time: 10
  minutes
Serves 6
EASY

½ *sheet focaccia bread
  measuring
  approximately
  40 cm x 40 cm*
3 tablespoons olive oil
175 g butter, softened
4 fillets anchovies
4 cloves garlic, crushed
*3 tablespoons finely
  chopped fresh basil
  leaves*
*3 tablespoons finely
  chopped fresh flat-leaf
  parsley*
*1 teaspoon ground black
  pepper*
½ *cup grated parmesan
  cheese*

1 Slit bread horizontally
in half. Place cut side up
on a flat tray. Drizzle
both halves with olive oil.
2 Cream butter with
anchovies, garlic, basil,
parsley and black
pepper. Spread each side
of the bread with half
the butter. Sprinkle with
cheese.
3 Cook at 180°C for 10
minutes or until butter
and cheese melt and
brown lightly. Serve hot,
cut in squares.
Note: Focaccia is sold in
large flat sheets by the
quarter, half or whole. If
unavailable use 2 cm
slices of Italian bread.

Italian Bread

HINT
Continental parsley is
a flat-leaf variety,
which has a strong
distinct flavour.
Curly-leaved parsley
is an acceptable
substitute.

HINT
When chopping fresh
chillies, it is best to
use rubber gloves to
protect hands. If you
handle fresh chillies
with your hands,
avoid touching the
face or eyes, since
painful burning will
occur.